# Visible

# Scars

*Healing the Pain*

# VISIBLE SCARS
## *Healing the Pain*

**By:** *Nikki Hancheck*

Printed in the United States of America
ISBN: 978-0988718838

# *Dedication*

This book is dedicated to my two wonderful
daughters. It is my hope you don't go through
all I've been through. I spent most of my life
with my head down, being quiet and trying to
fit into places I was not designed to fit in.  I
allowed myself to lose so much sight of who I
was, I became someone I didn't even
recognize.  I didn't have the strength or the
courage to be satisfied with who I truly am,
but I soon realized God is not the author of
confusion.  Please keep this in mind, always
follow your heart, pray and know that God
will always lead you to places where
happiness and peace can finally be found.

# Table of Contents

# *Foreword*

Nikki is a strong, charismatic and beautiful woman. Her spirit always shines as the life of every gathering. She is a fighter. She loves hard and has a strong sense of family. This book is written to share firsthand experiences that have created some of her most visible scars. Her purpose is to help heal and to be healed. You will find her honesty and accountability to be a beautiful start to her healing process and is the key to any healing process. We love her for every perfect imperfection and applaud her for finally finding her voice.

*Porscha Hicks-Plant*

# *Introduction*

## *Is Giving Up An Option?*

"Just give up... I mean, if you keep going, you're only going to endure more pain, more rejection, more mistreatment, and disrespect... just quit Nikki... QUIT!" My mind was playing tricks on me, taunting me daily. Life has been having its way with me, and I haven't yet crossed the threshold to thirty. But, I refuse to give up. Life should never be so hard that giving up becomes an option; in which you find yourself holding a gun — not for protection, but — to end your life. Pain should never take hold of a soul like that. But it has me.

The first step in healing the most painful parts of oneself is telling yourself the truth. Truth is, I am still hurting, but I want to be healed and whole. That would not have been a true statement six months ago. Today, I want to be free of the burdens of every experience that left me scarred, angry, suffering, and feeling worthless.

I now realize that accomplishing these things could not (would not) happen without letting my guard down and letting God in. So, take a walk with me. This is an invitation into my life's journey toward healing, in *real time*. In this book, I've chosen to share my journey with the world, in hopes that it will encourage whomever reads it. Thank you for taking this walk with me. *Ready? Get set ... GO!!!*

# *Chapter One...*

*The Scrapes of Rejection*

I was born November 16, 1987 in Colorado Springs, Colorado, the second of my mother's three children. My sister Shay is two years older than me, and my brother James is three years my junior. My siblings and I did not share the same father; and my mother did not know who mine was.

My grandmother was my mother's sole support system, and she had already been raising Shay when I came along. Following my birth, my mother served my grandmother a promise that "she would do better by me;" better than she had done by Shay. When I was older, my grandmother expressed to me the she always had hope in those empty declarations, even though she somehow knew that nothing would come of them.

My mother's Achilles heel was drugs and alcohol. Her addiction was one of the many crutches she used to avoid facing the true essence of her pain: her need and desire to be loved. My mother had no clue what to do with me. It was nothing for her to put beer in one of my sippy cups, and full meals came far and few between.

I lived with my mother for the first four years of my life and, when I turned three, she gave birth to my little brother James.

I was in the care of others quite often within those four years; some whom my mother knew, some she didn't. I remember one person, whose name was Steve, who was in and out of our home a lot. He was an older, malnourished, white man with missing teeth. My mother left me in his care often and I would always have fun with him. We'd play at the pool and eat lots of pizza.

Steve wanted to make sure I was comfortable with him before he robbed me of every ounce of innocence I had. Shortly after I began to feel safe with him, Steve began molesting me. My excitement to go with him when my mother had "somewhere to be" turned into fits and pleas for her not to leave me with him. But she was so consumed with her own desires, she didn't notice anything wrong. This is when I began to cleave to dysfunction and embrace abuse. I simply didn't know any better.

My mother's having chosen men, alcohol, and drugs over my siblings and I was the seed that gave root to my insecurities. But, there is nothing purer than a child's love. No

12

matter how many times my mother messed up, I gave her a chance. I needed her love. I wanted her affection and I wanted her to want me.

I loved my mother unconditionally. I didn't care if she was high or passed-out drunk. I still wanted her around. In my mind, what I experienced at the hands of my mother was love; and, as I grew and others treated me in similar ways, I accepted it as love, too.

But no matter how much love I held in my heart for my mother, it wasn't enough to keep her around. Her desire to feed her addiction meant more to her than seeing my siblings and I grow up.

I remember the day she walked away. My grandmother had come to pick us up. I sat in the back of her care with Shay and James, who was in a car seat. The ride to our destination was quiet. I wasn't sure where we were going, but I was glad we were all together. Shay and I played in the back while my mother sat in the front passenger seat, staring out of the window, and my grandmother drove along silently.

We pulled up to a bus station and my mother got out of the car and went into the bus station. My grandmother removed luggage from the trunk, ushered us out of the car, and we all waited for my mother to return.

My mother came rushing out of the bus station, and came over to hug us. When I saw Steve come up behind her and grab her bag, I got excited, thinking we were all getting ready to go with her. I hurried, hugged my grandmother, Shay and James and rushed off behind her. But, my mother stopped me.

"No Honey, Mommy's the only one going. You're going to stay with your grandmother. I love you all, but I have to go with Steve. I love him too much not to."

I stood there — sick and in complete shock, I couldn't believe my mother just walked away. My grandmother hugged me and put us all back in the car, where I cried the entire ride home.

"Ain't no use crying over things you can't control" my grandmother said.

I remember feeling like the wind had been knocked out of me. There was an overwhelming sense of loneliness … rejection. I couldn't understand why my

mother didn't want me. I found myself
asking a lot of questions on the inside. What
had I done wrong? Was I a bad child? Was
I ugly? Did I hurt her? The seed of
insecurity was now a tree; and it was
steadily growing.

# *Chapter Two...*

*Scrapes Turned Cuts*

My grandmother was now raising my siblings and me, and one of my aunts. She amazed me. Not many people would do what she did. I often find myself imagining the strength it took for her to care for us and deal with my mother's issues. She mothered and loved us with everything in her; but there is something about the love of the woman you came from that is so powerful, that I don't think many understand the type of void that leaves when it is not there.

One thing I remember vividly about my grandmother was how much she prayed. I really didn't understand why she always had to "talk to Jesus." I had no clue who Jesus was, and I was too scared to ask her, because I didn't want her talking to Him about me.

My grandmother had us in church four out of seven days a week (laughing to myself). I didn't understand why we had to be there, but I would learn that much later.

I was still struggling with my mother not being around and, although I could depend on my grandmother and tell her anything, I didn't know how to tell her that I really just wanted my mother. I didn't want to hurt my grandmother's feelings. I knew how hard she worked to take care of us. I didn't want to be unfair.

It was in this place where my void-filling began; where I began my search for love and acceptance. I knew I was loved, but something was missing. I had a deep-rooted longing that couldn't be filled by those around me. How many of you know that, when you have a need, a natural, but essential need, when you don't know any better, you'll accept anything that comes close?

I believe I was about nine years old when, one Sunday at the end of service, my grandmother decided that we would join the church we had been attending in Denver. I remember us all leaving our seats and walking together to the altar. It seemed like the longest walk ever to get to the front of the church.

When we got to the altar, I looked up to see a tall, dark, beautiful man in a long white robe standing before me — the pastor of the church. If I had to describe him, I would say he resembled former NBA player Antonio McDyess.

This pastor was my first crush. I remember being excited to attend church just to see him. He and his wife would allow me to hang out with them and he even started calling me his little daughter.

At the time, I had no real sense of the spirit that was finding a resting place in my young impressionable soul, but something was taking root.

As I grew into adolescence, I became aware of my sexuality and the attention I was getting from men. I had a lot of "crushes" on men in pastoral positions, which was rooted in need for parental love and acceptance. There was something about a "man of God," that intrigued me; the power and the influence did something to me.

My grandmother would have many conversations with me about God, His Word and how He would not be mocked. I would nod in agreement, but her words often went into one ear and out of the other and, as I grew, I began acting on my attraction to pastors. Those puppy dog crushes I had on men in leadership came to a natural reality around the age of 16.

A youth pastor at a church I'd visited took an interest in me. He was ten years my senior. I knew my grandmother wouldn't have a problem with me going to church, so that was how I got to see him. I went to "church" a lot.

My experience with that pastor was my first real "situation;" my first sexual encounter, and it resulted in my contracting an STD. I was hurt and angry, and I wanted to scratch his face off when I stood in the doctor's office and learned the news. But, I didn't have the strength to confront him. And I was too ashamed to tell my grandmother whom I had contracted it from. It was bad enough that she had to find out I was sexually active in such a way.

I never heard from that pastor again. He got what he wanted and bounced. This was when I learned how to suppress and numb pain.

At age 17, a 42-year-old married pastor heavily pursued me; often telling me the ungodly things he wanted to do with me. I never allowed anything to materialize between us. I used to talk to him often until things got really weird between us. He'd made it clear that he wanted to have sex with me.  I stopped all communication with him and that's when the craziness started.  He would show up at my school unannounced, attend my basketball games and even come by my house and sit outside my window.  After I threatened to call the police, he left me alone.

I finally turned 18 and, being of legal age, it felt like the world was my oyster.  I started dating a pastor who was 30 years older than me.  I was attracted to the illusion of power his "position" presented, so I dismissed all the perfectly placed red flags.  He was almost 50, still living with his momma, and now dating an 18-year-old girl.  He played on my insecurities and I did not value myself enough to know that the entire situation was wrong.  I didn't know much about *daddy issues*, but I was plagued with them.

I wanted love, but my quest was fueled by lust.  I measured the quality of a man by what he looked like, how much money he had and his social status. A recipe for disaster.  In the early era of social media, the *MySpace* days, I caught the attention of a guy named Jay.  Jay and I would spend hours online chatting, and eventually exchanged numbers.  Our online chats turned to hours of conversations, until we met in person.

Jay swept me off my feet. We were dated for a little over six months when I became pregnant.

To be honest, Jay and I really didn't know anything about each other; but, in an effort to do the right thing, we decided to get married. My grandmother was dead set against it, and I even ignored the internal indicators that warned me not.

Jay and I had a small courthouse ceremony, with his mother and my grandmother as the witnesses to our union. The ceremony seemed more like a technicality. We stood before the judge, said our "I Do's," gave each other a small peck on the lips at the close, and the two of us went right back to at our jobs.

Shortly after our nuptials, I gave birth to Layla — a beautiful baby girl. I was 20 years old.

My marriage was transactional. Jay and I worked and ran the home, but we weren't growing together. We still knew very little about one another. Early in our marriage,

Jay enlisted in the army. Our marriage lasted seven years. Jay was deployed most of the time, which is why I think we were together for as long as we were. However, not too long after he returned from one of his tours, our marriage ended. While away, Jay had carried on a full-fledge affair. I discovered this when I happened upon some pictures and videos that he was bold enough to leave on his laptop for me to see.

Jay's cheating sparked an anger in me, the likes of which I had never felt before. All I could see was red. Even though our marriage was more of a *roommates-with-benefits* arrangement, I had always been faithful. But Jay's cheating awoke something in me; a vengeful temperament. I wanted him to hurt as much as he'd hurt me.

And the only thing I could think of to hurt him more would be to cheat on him. Now, I know you must be thinking, *"Why would that hurt him if you all weren't in love in the first place?"* Well, if I knew anything about Jay, it was that he was territorial. He may not have loved me but, in his mind, I was his and, if I gave what was his to someone else, it would hurt him deep. It was in this period of my life that I learned just how many of my mother's issues I had inherited.

I can recall having many casual sexual encounters and justifying them with "*This is hurting Jay;*" all while destroying *me*. This wasn't what I wanted. I wanted to be loved for me, not my body.

I decided to leave Jay but, by the time I did, I was a mental wreck. I'd come to the realization that my life was eerily mirroring that of my mother's; which further pushed me down that toxic road. I had too much pride to tell my grandmother what I was going through. When I called or stopped by, she would always tell me that she was praying for me. To this day, I'm sure my grandmother knew what I was going through, but all she could do was pray. My life was out of her control.

*Visible Scars*

# *Chapter Three...*

*Cuts to Bruises*

I played with a lot of hearts after my marriage with Jay ended. I would enter into relationships under the pretense that I was looking for love, knowing that wasn't the case. I wasn't looking for love, because love wasn't what I thought I needed during that time. I wanted to be taken care of without too much expectation of reciprocation.

I ended up meeting a guy on my job: Jacob. I believe Jacob knew he was dealing with a wounded woman, because he played me, played with me, and played on me, causing me some of my deepest pain. It's funny, I put my heart, soul and desires into yet another toxic relationship — and my relationship with Jacob was indeed toxic. I loved him with all of me, and he cheated on me for most of our relationship. I was hurt, but I was desperate to have him in my life, so I stayed.

I soon became pregnant and I remember Jacob being so upset. He told me that children weren't in his plans and he asked me to abort the baby. I wanted him to know that I love him and that, if that was what he wanted, I would do it. I had the abortion, even though everything in me was telling me not to do it. I went through this cycle with Jacob twice.

How could it be so easy for him to ask me to abort our children, without a thought? He had no regard for the endless tears I cried; the emotional pain I was in. I developed a heavy drinking habit; occasionally popping pills to cope with the emotional pain of the abortions. My drinking landed me in the ER with alcohol poisoning on three separate occasions.

I was in a terrible place. I couldn't care for Layla like she needed, so I allowed Jay to take custody of her while I worked on getting myself together. Giving Jay custody of Layla was one of the toughest things I ever had to do. The memory of my mother walking away from me played over and over in my head.

I made a commitment to Layla that I loved her and would never be far from her. I fought hard to make sure she knew that I wasn't abandoning her and that I was here for her. When we were children, my grandmother would say, "*An empty mind is the devil's playground. When you are not thinking on the things of God, you make room for Satan to play.*"

Well, she was right. Satan had a field day playing in my head on the day I decided to give Jay full custody of Layla. He would whisper to me, "*It's inevitable. You're destined to be just like your mother.*"

I began drinking even more. I felt like I was on a winding dark road with no light in sight.

I didn't like being alone. The silence was deafening. And I didn't give myself a chance to process all that I'd gone through up to this point. In true Nikki fashion, I bandaged my scars with another relationship.

This guy's name was Tim. The premise of our relationship was rickety from the jump. It was purely sexual. Tim gave me one of the most intense sexual experiences of my life. I was so taken by how he made me feel, I ignored every sign that was telling me he's not the one.

Here's a nice side-note about lust, "IT WILL BLIND YOU."

My relationship with Tim was tumultuous, and extremely dysfunctional. My family did not approve, but I listened to no one but

Nikki. I was intoxicated with Tim. He was like a drug. Again, I ended up pregnant, and soon gave birth to another baby girl — Daiza.

Once again, my grandmother shared her truth with me.

"This isn't the path you should go down baby. He isn't the one for you."

I didn't listen to her, and I know it may seem like God was far away from me during this time, but He wasn't, I just wasn't trying to hear Him either. I may have been able to dismiss my grandmother's warnings, but God... He does NOT play that. God was finally like, "Fine. If you are not going to listen, then I'm going to show you."

One Saturday evening, I stayed after work and had a couple of shots with the crew. We hung out until about 4:30am. When we finally decided to head home for the night, I got in my car and headed down the tollway, the quickest way home.

It was really dark and there were limited street lights. I remember the song *Studio* coming on, and I began to doze off. I kept dozing and waking up. I decided to roll

down the windows to keep me awake. I
rolled down all four windows and turned the
music on blast. That lasted all of 30
seconds. I again dozed off — this time for a
while — and I could feel the car drifting and
slowing down; but, when I was finally fully
awake, it was too late. The car had veered
off the road and was skidding, seconds from
hitting a guard rail. To avoid the collision, I
jerked the steering wheel to the right and
slid across the road. I remember feeling like
*This is it. If you're going to take me God,
I'm ready.*

The car flipped about three times, ending up
on a hill on the right side of the street. I
don't remember feeling anything, because
my body was so relaxed. I do remember
seeing black and white lights behind my
closed eyes.

When I woke up, I was in the back seat.
There was no way I should have survived. I
believe God wanted to give me a wakeup
call, but not allow me to die.

I was confused when I fully came to. I
looked up and saw that the engine was
smoking, so I hurried out of the car. I made
my way to the street to try and flag someone

down, but there was hardly anyone on the road that early in the morning.

I finally saw a car coming. I tried yelling for help, but nothing would come out of my mouth. I attempted to wave my arms, but my left arm would not move. Somehow the driver of the car saw me and pulled over to the side of the road. I was still in so much shock that I didn't know what was going on.

The police and EMTs showed up. They placed me on a gurney and loaded me into the back of the ambulance, all the while asking me a million questions.

Once I arrived at the hospital, I just knew I was going to jail or detox for drinking and driving. One of the police officers from the scene was there, he waited for the ER doctors to finish examining me before he spoke with me.

I remember crying and addressing him with "Yes, Sir," and "No, Sir."

"You seem like a good person, and from your record, you're never in trouble. You just had a really bad night," He said. "I'm not going to take you in. I will drop all of the pending charges, except driving under the influence."

The strangest thing happened after that. He asked if he could pray for me. This was God — I mean — come on! Who has ever heard of a police officer dropping rightly deserved charges of an offender with whom he has no allegiance, and then offering to pray for them?

The officer prayed for me and told me he would continue to pray for me. He then called my grandparents to pick me up.

Now, did I listen to God after that humbling experience and leave my situation — get my life together? No. I desperately wanted to prove everyone wrong and show them that this was my family. I loved Tim and I loved Daiza. The way my pride was set up, was I refuse to fail. We were a family, and I was determined to make it work.

In recounting my journey, one thing I truly appreciate is the faithfulness of God, despite my slip-ups, He never left me.

# *Chapter Four...*

*Bruised and Broken*

In an effort to prove a point to my family and everyone that disagreed with my relationship with Tim, I dismissed very present warning signs. Tim never held a job, but he always had money. And even though everything in me was telling me to question it, I didn't. I later found that Tim was involved in various types of fraud; but my allegiance to him was so deep-rooted that, when the Feds wanted me to come down and talk about him, I wouldn't. In an effort to stay under the radar, Tim decided we should move. So, Tim, Daiza and I relocated to Dallas, Texas.

Upon moving to Dallas, we joined a church. Tim and I served there, and I continued to try to convince my family and myself that what we had was legitimate. Shortly after our move, Tim and I married. I didn't pray on it and I really wasn't listening for anything that went against what I wanted. It was in this season of my life that I learned the most about self-indulgence and how much my choices shaped the condition my life was in.

Tim and I were poisoning each other. We both continuously disrespected the sanctity of our marriage and ended up separating. Tim stopped attending our church while I continued on and, in my mind, I thought, *"I'm attending church every Sunday, serving and acknowledging God. I'm doing what I'm supposed to be doing so I'm good."*

If you take nothing else away from this, I hope you gather that attending church doesn't make you any more in tune with God than standing in one place makes you a statue. It isn't *the going* that produces results; it's listening, sacrificing, taking responsibility, accountability, prayer and obedience.

One Sunday during meet and greet, I met a guest pastor who'd spoken at the church a few times: Pastor Troy. We started out cordially. I'd greet him when I saw him and we would have small talk in the church lobby; but nothing more than that.

I found myself extremely attracted to Pastor Troy, and he wasn't shy about expressing his interest in me. Now, one would think, this is a married "man of God," and he is in full pursuit of you — RUN GIRL, RUN!!

Unfortunately, it didn't go down like that; Pastor Troy fed my ego, serving as a yet another filler. He told me all the things I wanted to hear. He was good-looking, well-known; and the most attractive thing about him, to me, was that he was a minister. I was still blind to my current state, and my marriage was the furthest thing from my mind. I was even entertaining the idea of this being my chance to become a First Lady.

The cycle of relationships between pastors and me started up again and, this time, it came back with full force. Pastor Troy was 20 years my senior, lived in a different state and, of course, I was completely married. But I still walked around unbothered by how all-wrong we were.

I traveled to other states with Pastor Troy while he preached. He would fly to Dallas and we would spend time together. By all accounts I was his woman. However, in God's Eyes, I was completely out of order.

There was no balance in my relationship with Pastor Troy. We were either extremely calm or a complete tsunami. Every time I felt he wasn't doing things the way I wanted, I blew up and hurled anger-fueled words at him. There was never a medium and there never was going to be.

Pastor Troy had had enough of my outbursts, and suggested I get counseling. Now, that would have been a good idea, if counseling was what I wanted. But, deep down, I didn't. I agreed to counseling because I loved him.

I attended session after session with a therapist, pouring my heart out, sharing my life story from the rejection of my mother and not knowing my father to molestation, almost being raped by a former high school teacher, abortions, relationships, drinking, drugging, partying — all of it

I spilled; but one thing I had not done yet was face God.

I've taken enough falls to now know I need to face the woman in the mirror. And that has not been easy. Counseling was a great start. It is still very much a work in progress; however, I don't dismiss the fact that I have come pretty far.

I ended up walking away from Pastor Troy, too. I found myself thinking, "*Maybe being in a relationship just isn't for me.*" Relationships seemed to be more of a distraction. But, being alone may have been the best thing for my daughters and me.

I needed to get back to me. As you have read, I'm most comfortable in patterns that often prove to be unhealthy. Attention is my weakness. It was the thing I lacked the most growing up and the desire for it followed me into adulthood. But I am determined to break that stronghold.

# *Chapter Five...*

*Pained...All Bled Out*

Tim decided he wanted to mend our marriage, while mending anything with him was the last thing on my mind. I couldn't see myself doing it all over again, but I gave it a try. For Daiza's sake — the chance of her being happy and growing up with two parents – I decided to go one more time with Tim.

We agreed to meet with a marriage counselor in the local area. I found myself intrigued by the counselor. I was less and less concerned about what he could do to help my marriage and more concerned about him — who he was, what he was about and how I could get to know him better. I grew fond of him with every session we had. I hung on his every word and looked forward to him sharing his insight.

The sessions soon took a turn. Tim and I were attending them less and less, but we both continued to communicate with the counselor individually. He and Tim forged a friendship, while he and I were forging a more intimate relationship.

If Tim knew that his new "best friend" was secretly taking his wife right from under him, he would have gone crazy on him.

An entire year passed and the counselor and
I had developed a routine. We would meet at
our spot every week to have drinks,
spending a lot of time just enjoying each
other's company. I became so wrapped up
in this man — almost to the point that my
every thought was of him.

I not only invested my time, but money and,
eventually, my body came into the equation.
It was as if I were under a spell. I mean this
man had all my attention and, sadly, all of
me. I was convinced he could do no wrong
and then one night, everything I thought he
was flew out of the window.

He took advantage of me. He disrespected
me in a way that I honestly don't even have
the words to articulate it. I thought he loved
me, I thought I was important to him,
someone he cared for. I found out that, to
him, I meant nothing. He raped me. He used
me, hurt me, and left me for emotional
death.

And yet, there I stood, still in love with this
man. Even after scarring me the way he did,
I didn't want anything bad to happen to him.
I decided to let it go, but at the expense of
myself (once again). I began drinking again
and, to numb the pain even more, I added

painkillers to the cocktail. I did whatever I could to suppress what happened to me. I had to bury the guilt and shame of simply *letting it go.*

I suffered in agony for days, my body aching and my heart full of sorrow. I decide to go home to my family. As soon as I got off the plane, I saw my sister at the gate. I immediately begin to cry and she ran to me, grabbed and hugged me. I arrived at my grandparents' home, and they were waiting up to talk to me. I shared with them what happened, and my grandfather kept his head down so that I couldn't see his expression. He eventually left the room and didn't return that evening.

My grandmother and sister did not understand why I didn't pressed charges. My sister urged me to get a rape kit, but I was so afraid. I took up for him.

The rape took place in March of this year, 2017. As I write, I still cry, still hurt. But, as crazy as this may sound, I am humbled. I am humble enough to want better for myself; to see God beyond the religious box I'd placed Him in. I want to be better, I want to be healed,

I AM NOT my mother. I want the holes in my soul and in my heart to be filled by God entirely.

*Visible Scars*

# Chapter Six...

*The Road to Healing*

I am on the road to recovery. I decided it was time to stop playing games. Tim and I are finally working out our divorce. I am getting individual counseling and working hard to face the demons I've suppressed for so long. How else will I defeat them if I don't face them? I made intentional choices that should have cost me my life; however, I have learned something more about Grace.

I had a transparent conversation with my family, which was a pivotal point for me on this journey. I am taking time to get to know me, forgiving myself and praying forgiveness from God and the people I've hurt. God is doing a lot of delayering, and that process has its pain, too, but I'd rather face the God-induced pain then the self-inflicted pain I've suffered over the past 29 years.

I realized through writing this book that I have to forgive my mother. Her addiction is still priority one in her life and I'd be lying if I didn't say I have some hardened spots in my own heart as a result. But, in order for me to move forward, I have to forgive her, I have to find it in my heart to sincerely pray for her.

I no longer take on the burdens of my mother's issues. I am no longer reciting the mantra, "*I am my mama's baby, destined to be just like her.*"

I want to encourage you to listen for God, listen to God. Don't wait for Him to humble. You don't want that.

I take responsibility for the choices I made that landed me in many of the situations I was in, and I also know fully that the things others did to me are not mine to own. That rape was NOT MY FAULT, the molestation was NOT MY FAULT, and the rejection was NOT MY FAULT.

I was spiritually paralyzed for months after the rape, but I have decided to stand up for myself, I cannot let the pains of my past win. This fight is so much bigger than me. I have no choice but to lean on God, trust Him, and walk through this storm with Him.

For every woman who has been violated, mistreated, and mismanaged in life, I fight. I must fight for my daughters, fight that the curses I accepted onto myself from my mother are broken off their lives. I am fighting for the integrity of God's House;

because how men play with Him and His people is unfair.

I have a greater purpose, and I can make choices that will result in better outcomes.

You have an immeasurable value, that no relationship, no job title, no social status can define. Your value requires you to push through, knowing that God cares about everything concerning you.

If you pray, please continue to pray for me as I fight this very real and present battle for my life.

I hope that you will be encouraged to fight for that which had (*maybe still has*) a hold on you.

## *From My Heart To Yours*

I would be remiss not to thank you, the reader, for spending your money to buy this book and taking your precious time to read it — it means more than I can say. As stated previously, it is my hope that you are encouraged and inspired by all that I've written here, and that it even instills a call to action to embrace hurting people.

If you see the signs, don't ignore them. Don't judge them. Help them. If I could, I would destroy the roads I walked down if it meant that no one would endure the pain I did ever again. There are so many people suppressing their pain — pain so deeply hidden that they have no way of knowing the root cause of their issues — which results in their lives spinning out of control.

The world outside your window impacts your household and future, too. I can use the pain of my past and present to heal and help. And so can you.

Thank you for your support.

*Nikki*

## ***Connect With The Author***

Website:
https://www.followinghisway.com/author_nikki_hancheck.html

Email: authornikkihancheck@gmail.com

Facebook:
https://www.facebook.com/authornikkih/

@authornikkihancheck

Following His Way Publishing is a creative collective company that works with a large network of editors, graphic artists and marketing professionals to publish high quality projects for our customers. We seek to empower every author that we serve, whether it be in our end-to-end publishing of their book or providing consultation services providing free resources to assist them with self-publishing. Our ultimate goal is to produce professional products and providing top-notch service 100% of the time.

Interested in learning more? Contact us today at info@followinghisway.com.

Visit Us On The Web: https://www.followinghisway.com/fhw_writing_services.html

Let's connect on Social Media!

@followinghisway

*We look forward to serving you!*